Sparky
He is our pet

Sherry Ramrattan Smith and Benjamin Eric Smith

AuthorHouse™
1663 Liberty Drive
Bloomington, IN 47403
www.authorhouse.com
Phone: 1-800-839-8640

First published by AuthorHouse 4/1/2010

ISBN: 978-1-4490-9849-0 (sc)

Library of Congress Control Number: 2010903431

Printed in the United States of America
Bloomington, Indiana

This book is printed on acid-free paper.

authorHOUSE®

For

Madyn

Sparky is six weeks old.
He comes to our home to live with us.

We teach Sparky his name.
When we call him, he listens.

At bedtime, Sparky goes to his kennel to sleep.
He likes to have his favorite toys with him.

Sparky enjoys being outside.
Sometimes we give him treats
and teach him tricks.

He is very cuddly.
Sparky likes to be hugged.

On warm days, Sparky likes to lie in the shade.
He keeps his favorite toy close by.

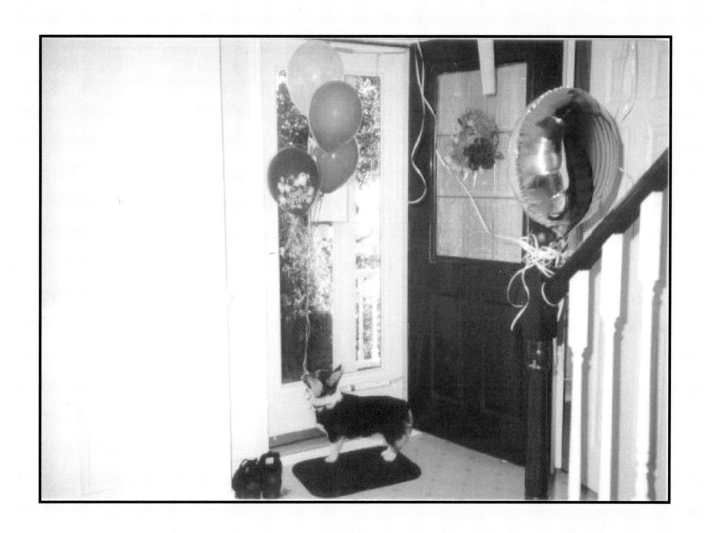

Sparky helps us to celebrate special occasions.
He carries balloons for a party.

Sparky grows into a smart and handsome dog.
He is always alert.

As he grows up, Sparky learns how to swim.
He likes to swim in the lake.

Sparky plays with his new ball.
He wears his favorite sports jersey.

Sparky likes squeaky toys.
He plays with a new one he got for his birthday.

When Sparky wants to go outside,
he goes to the door.
When he wants to come back into the house,
he calls us by barking at the window.

Sparky is curious.
He wants to learn new things so he pays
attention when we speak to him.

Sparky loves walks.
We get ready to go outside together.

We walk Sparky at least two times each day.
This helps him to stay healthy.

Sparky wears a clown hat for Halloween.
He greets children when they come to the door.

Sparky also has a house outside.
Sometimes he likes to take a nap in his house.

On his birthday, he enjoys a special treat.
Sparky is a happy dog.

Sparky loves the snow.
His fur coat keeps him warm.

Sparky has his own Christmas stocking.
He waits patiently to see what's inside.

Sparky takes a rest when he is tired.
He likes to lie on his back with
his feet in the air.

Sparky enjoys family vacations.
We love Sparky.

About Sparky

Sparky is a tri-color, Pembroke Welsh Corgi. He was born on February 22, 2002 in Wellesley, Ontario. He lives with Sherry, Brian, Ben, and Matthew in Waterloo, Ontario, Canada.

A Considerate Curriculum

Curriculum is about choices we make every day. A *Considerate Curriculum* encourages us to critically examine our actions and carefully consider how our interactions can be supportive and nurturing.